NOT NOW DEAR !

TO MUM

NOT NOW DEAR!

JOHN ASTROP

Patrick Hardy Books

PATRICK HARDY BOOKS
28 Percy Street, London
W1P 9FF, UK.

ISBN 0 7444 0023 6

ACKNOWLEDGMENT

The author and publisher are grateful to
Pan Books Ltd. for the use of a few of the
cartoons in this book which first appeared
in 1981 in a book which they published
called "Sun Child Moon Child" by John Astrop.

Printed in Great Britain

" IN THE LITTLE WORLD IN WHICH CHILDREN
HAVE THEIR EXISTENCE, WHOSOEVER BRINGS
THEM UP, THERE IS NOTHING SO FINELY
PERCEIVED AND SO FINELY FELT, AS INJUSTICE. "

CHARLES DICKENS - 'GREAT EXPECTATIONS'

"WE'VE SKRIMPED AND SAVED JUST TO GIVE YOU
ALL THE THINGS WE NEVER HAD...WHAT THANKS
DO WE GET? DON'T YOU **WANT** TO LOOK PRETTY?"

...AND IF YOU DON'T COME OUT OF THERE SOON YOU'LL
GET STUCK TO THAT SEAT AND WE'LL HAVE TO....

"FISH FINGERS O.K. FOR **YOU** GERALDINE?"

" WHY DO YOU HAVE TO COPY EVERYTHING THAT SILLY
KEVIN DOES...?WHY CAN'T YOU THINK FOR YOURSELF?
... AND BE MORE LIKE ROBERT!! "

"OH! THIS IS COLIN ... I DIDN'T REALISE HE WAS ...
ER ... TALLER THAN YOU!"

"OH DON'T WORRY – HE NEVER HEARS A THING THAT'S GOING ON AROUND HIM!"

" BUT DARLING THIS ONE IS THE VERY **BEST** !
YOU DON'T WANT THE SAME OLD ONE THAT
ALL THE OTHERS HAVE GOT DO YOU ? "

"YOU **TOLD** ME YOU DIDN'T HAVE HOMEWORK!"

" THOUSANDS OF POOR LITTLE CHILDREN IN THE
WORLD TODAY ARE STARVING...AND **YOU** WON'T
EAT UP YOUR CRISPY COD FRIES !!! "

"NOW COME ON YOU TWO, ACT SENSIBLY LIKE GROWN UP PEOPLE AND **STOP** BICKERING!"

" OF COURSE YOU CAN CHOOSE FOR YOURSELF...
NO...NOT **THAT** ONE DARLING... "

"YOU'LL **THANK** US LATER FOR MAKING YOU PRACTISE!"

" I EXPECT DADDY WAS BUSY AND DIDN'T KNOW
YOU'D MADE SUCH A LOVELY PATTERN FOR HIM
... OH MY GOD ! THE POOLS COUPON ! "

"WELL YOU'LL **HAVE** TO WEAR IT WHEN GRANNIE COMES ON SUNDAY!"

"HE WASN'T TOO KEEN AT FIRST,
BUT WE TALKED IT OVER, MAN TO MAN,
AND I THINK THE LITTLE BEGGAR'S
BEGINNING TO SEE IT MY WAY!"

"NOT **NOW** DEAR, YOU KNOW DADDY DOESN'T LIKE YOU TO HAVE THE TRAIN SET OUT 'TIL HE GETS HOME .... OF COURSE IT'S YOURS DARLING .... BUT..."

"**GOOD LAD**! TUCK IN...THAT'LL PUT HAIR ON YOUR CHEST!"

"IF YOU DO THAT JUST **ONCE** MORE...**OK** JUST DO IT AGAIN
THAT'S ALL ....**RIGHT** THE NEXT TIME YOU DO IT THERE'LL BE
TROUBLE....**NOW** YOU'VE DONE IT....I SHAN'T TELL YOU AGAIN
....**RIGHT**... "

"JUST WAIT 'TIL I GET YOU HOME, YOU LITTLE DEVIL."

"NO DARLING!
- MUMMY REALLY WOULD PREFER THE **TOP** ONE!"

" I WON'T HAVE BULLYING IN **MY** HOUSE,
JUST TO GET YOUR OWN WAY!
IF YOU DON'T STOP RIGHT NOW
I'LL GIVE YOU SUCH A WALLOPING! "

" YOU'VE GOT A CHEEK YOUNG MADAM,
IF I DIDN'T HAVE A BUNCH OF KIDS
I WOULDN'T **NEED** TO SMOKE ! "

ROBERT! WHAT ON EARTH DID YOU HAVE IN YOUR POCKET!"

" NO MY LOVE, COURSE CATS CAN'T FLY."

" I REALLY DON'T KNOW DEAR, ARITHMETIC SEEMS TO BE QUITE DIFFERENT NOWADAYS ! "

"... IF I COME UP THERE AND FIND IT MY GIRL ...
THERE'S GOING TO BE REAL TROUBLE !
AND **DON'T** MAKE THAT ROOM IN A MESS !!

" OH **MY** GOD . . . ER . . . WHAT A LOVELY PRESENT. "

" OK KIDS, EGG AND WATERCRESS SANDWICHES FIRST!"

"**AIN'T! AIN'T!** WHAT KIND OF ENGLISH D'THEY LEARN YOU AT SCHOOL!"

"...YES DARLING - MUMMY'LL HAVE A LOOK AT THE
FUNNY WORM WHEN SHE'S FINISHED WHAT SHE'S DOING."

"THEY'RE NOT REALLY SPOOKY DARLING,
WE'VE **ALL** GOT ONE INSIDE US!"

" **HANKIE!** JUSTIN...OH LORD ANOTHER SNAIL TRAIL."

"MUMMY'LL COME IN A MINUTE AND SEE THE LOVELY CAR YOU'VE PAINTED."

"IF YOU FALL DOWN AND BREAK A LEG, **DON'T** COME RUNNING TO ME!"

"WHAT DO YOU MEAN **YUK**!! WE WOULD GIVE ANYTHING FOR A STICK OF LIQUORICE WHEN WE WERE KIDS!"

" I DON'T KNOW **HOW** WE'RE GOING TO MAKE A MAN OF YOU,
ALWAYS WITH YOUR HEAD STUCK IN SOME BLOOMIN' BOOK
WHY DON'T YOU GET OUT AND KICK A BALL AROUND
LIKE A **REAL** LAD ? "

" WHY CAN'T YOU SETTLE DOWN AND READ A GOOD BOOK ?
LIFE ISN'T JUST BOOTING A **BALL** AROUND YOU KNOW!"

"HOW WAS I TO KNOW IT WAS **YOUR** EARWIG!!"

"DON'T BE SILLY DEAR, OF COURSE GUARDIAN ANGELS
HAVEN'T GOT CLAWS AND BIG BLACK TEETH ! "
... THAT'S WEREWOLVES !! "

" YOU DON'T WANT TO GROW UP TO BE A BIG MAN
WHO CAN'T **TIE** HIS LACES DO YOU ?

.... DON'T BE SILLY, BOYS **CAN'T** BE LITTLE LADIES. "

"... AND YOU'RE **NOT** TO EAT WHITE BREAD, WHITE SUGAR
NO DRINKS WITH ARTIFICIAL ADDITIVES... NO CRISPS ...
HAVE A LOVELY TIME DARLING ... AND **NO** CHOCOLATE AND ..."

"...YES, GAVIN HAS A HEART OF GOLD, BLESS HIM ...
SHARES **ALL** HIS TOYS WITH HIS LITTLE FRIENDS!"

" I DON'T KNOW WHAT THE FUNNY MONKEY'S DOING...
OH, **QUICK**, LOOK AT THE LOVELY BABY PANDA ! "

"... COMICS, COMICS, COMICS, YOU SEEM TO THINK WE'RE **MADE** OF MONEY!"

" DON'T BE SILLY DEAR, MUMMY JUST **HAD** TO WASH IT,
IT REALLY **DIDN'T** SMELL VERY NICE ! "

"BIG BOYS DON'T TAKE SILLY OLD TEDDIES TO SCHOOL!"

"NO DARLING, IT WOULDN'T HELP US TO BLOW-UP ALL THE PEOPLE WHO MAKE THE BOMBS .... WELL WE'D BE NASTY **THEN** WOULDN'T WE ?   NO DARLING, STRANGLING'S NASTY TOO... AND POISONING ... AND ... "

"DON'T BE SILLY CLIVE, IF YOU CAN'T SING YOUR LITTLE SONG FOR GRANNIE YOU **CERTAINLY** CAN'T HAVE THE LOVELY PRESENT THAT SHE BROUGHT FOR YOU..."

"**ADRIAN**, PLEASE **TRY** AND LOOK HAPPY!"

"ADAM ! IF YOU KEEP DOING **THAT**
IT'LL SHRIVEL UP AND FALL OFF ! "

"**O.K.** YOU LOT, **WHAT'S** GOING ON ....? HAVEN'T HEARD
A PEEP OUT OF YOU FOR TEN MINUTES....!"

"COMPLETE FREEDOM OF EXPRESSION, WE BELIEVE,
EXPANDS THE INDIVIDUALITY, AND ALLOWS THE CHILD
TO GROW CONFIDENTLY INTO A WHOLE PERSON . . . . .
BY THE WAY . . . ANYONE SEEN HIM TODAY ! "

"NOT **NOW** DEAR, MUMMY'S TIRED."

"EVERY TIME YOU TELL A LIE, GOD PUTS ANOTHER BLACK MARK IN HIS BIG BOOK - GOD DOESN'T LIKE PEOPLE WHO TELL LIES!"

" YOU JUST DON'T REALISE HOW RESTRICTING
KIDS CAN BE."

" FACE UP TO HIM LAD, ALL BULLIES ARE COWARDS,
JUST FACE UP TO HIM!"

"**LOOK** SWEETIE, GO AND BOTHER MUMMY!"

" SORRY DARLING, DADDY DIDN'T **KNOW** YOUR LITTLE FRIEND WAS SITTING HERE, I'M SURE FAIRIES CAN'T GET SQUASHED AND DEAD .... LOOK THERE SHE IS ....
.. OH FOR GOD'S SAKE, GO AND MAKE UP **ANOTHER** ONE ! "

" **ADAM** ...! YOU FORGOT MUMSIE'S LITTLE KISSY! "

" IF YOU'VE FINISHED WATCHING 'MAGIC HOUR'
SWITCH THAT DARNED TV OFF ! "

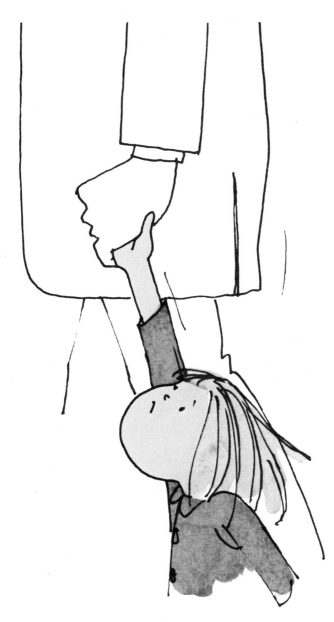

" NO I JUST CAN'T CARRY YOU LOVEY,
DADDY'S POOR ARMS ACHE!"

" ... AND THESE SCANDANAVIAN TOYS ARE SUCH BEAUTIFUL **BASIC** DESIGN, I MEAN, THEY REALLY ENCOURAGE THE CHILD TO USE HIS FULL IMAGINATIVE FACULTIES!"

" OF COURSE HE REMEMBERS HIS AUNTIE ROSE
DOESN'T HE !! "

"I DON'T KNOW WHERE YOU PICK UP THAT BLOODY LANGUAGE. YOU RUDE LITTLE BASTARD!"

.. AND EVERY FIVE MINUTES IT'S SWEETS, SWEETS, SWEETS!
WELL LET ME TELL YOU, LITTLE MADAM, THEY'RE BECOMING
A BAD HABIT AND THAT WON'T KEEP YOU HEALTHY AND ... "

"NOW GODFREY, GIVE YOUR LITTLE COUSIN A NICE BIG HUG!"

"OH NO WE WON'T TOLERATE AGRESSIVE WAR TOYS,
THANK GOODNESS FOR LEGO AND THE CONCEPT OF
BUILDING AS OPPOSED TO DESTROYING AND ... "

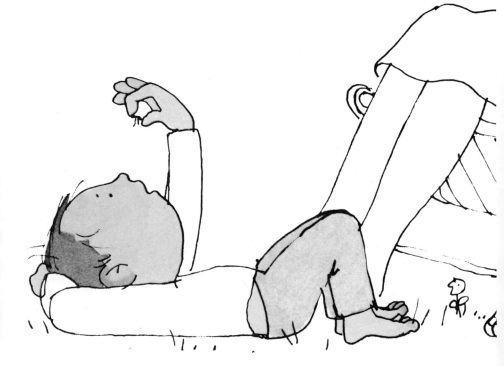

"WELL DARLING, PERHAPS THE LITTLE ANT HASN'T GOT ONE."

"I HAVEN'T GOT TIME TO ANSWER YOUR STUPID QUESTIONS
HOW THE HECK DO I KNOW WHO MADE GOD!!"

"OH, YES, EMILY, **VERY** LADYLIKE, I **MUST** SAY!"

"I'M REALLY WORRIED ABOUT HIM,
WITH SAGITTARIUS RISING, HE SHOULD BE
ADVENTUROUS, FUN-LOVING, FRANK,
PHILOSOPHICAL AND... WELL....! "

" THERE WE ARE DEAR – PACKED LUNCH READY –
CARROT AND LENTIL CROQUETTES, YOGHURT &
FROMENT – 'MM LOVELY – NOW RUN ALONG ... "

"NO DARLING, MUMMY WON'T BE CROSS...
MUMMY JUST WANTS YOU TO TELL THE TRUTH...
NOW COME ALONG TELL MUMMY...

... YOU LITTLE BUGGER I **KNEW** IT WAS YOU...!
JUST WAIT 'TIL YOUR FATHER ...."

" YOU HAVEN'T EATEN A THING SINCE THAT
BLASTED BIOLOGY LESSON . . . "

"DO TRY AND KEEP UP AMANDA WE'RE DOING THIS FOR YOU!"

"... WE'VE TRIED TO DISCOURAGE SEXIST ROLE-PLAYING AND IN FACT WILLIAM IS ~~HAPPIER~~ WITH DOLLS THAN HE IS WITH TRAINS!"

"WHAT DO YOU MEAN, THERE'S NOTHING TO DO WITH THEM?
LITTLE RUSSIAN CHILDREN SIMPLY **ADORE** THEM!"

"... I KNOW DEAR BUT IN SIX MONTHS TIME YOU'LL BE
AS BIG AS MARK ... "

" OF COURSE HE'S GOING TO KISS HIS NICE KIND AUNTIE,
HE KNOW'S THAT SILLY SHY BOYS DON'T GET
SPECIAL TREATS **EVER AGAIN !!** "

" WHAT THE HECK ARE **TWENTY HOLE D.M.'S**
WHEN THEY'RE AT HOME ! "

"**NO** CHRISTOPHER, WE **DON'T** WANT TO SEE IT DO WE.!!"

" I THINK WE'RE A BIT BIG FOR **KISSES** OLD CHAP !

. . . LET'S SHAKE HANDS. "

"NOW COME ALONG DEAR – E.T.'S GOING TO **DIE**
IF YOU DON'T OPEN THE SPACESHIP DOOR AND
LET HIM IN !! "

"OF COURSE I **KNOW** THE ANSWER, I JUST THINK
IT WOULD BE BEST IF YOU WORKED IT OUT YOURSELF."

"NEVER MIND **WHAT** LIVER IS, JUST EAT IT UP!"

"NOT NOW DEAR, DADDY'S BUSY!"

"I KNOW **I** SAID IT BUT IF I HEAR YOU SAY IT ONCE MORE YOU'LL BLOODY WELL COP IT MY LAD!"

"NO DARLING, I'M SURE GOD HAS GOT SOMETHING BETTER TO DO THAN WATCH **YOU** ON THE LOO!"

" NOT A **THOUGHT** FOR OTHER PEOPLE'S FEELINGS !! "

" ER...WE WERE JUST, ER ... CHANGING OVER SIDES ! "